VIOLINJUDY`S

A VIOLIN TREBLE

SUPPLEMENTARY SONGS AND ACTIVITIES
FOR BEGINNING THROUGH METHOD BOOK LEVEL 2
VIOLIN STUDENTS

VERY FUN VIOLIN COLLECTION

A Violin Treble by Judy Naillon

www.violinjudy.com
ISBN: 978-1-960674-15-9

Violin Judy's

VERY FUN VIOLIN LIBRARY

A Violin Treble is composed for violin students in levels C-D. Learners using this book should be able to hold the instrument up in playing position, understand a basic bow grip and have experience playing with fingers on the violin . A book level chart for the *Very Fun Violin Collection* is provided at the end of this book.

NOTE TO TEACHERS/PRACTICE PARENT:

Any beginning Violin Student can start in this book on a real instrument. For a total beginner ***A Violin Twinkle A*** will be a more helpful book to start! The pacing of this series is slower than any other method book you will find. This allows younger beginners time to really learn to read music as well as play a wide variety of songs. When you establish a firm foundation of technic, listening skills and songs students know and like to play, you'll have a violinist who learns to love music! Playing pieces that are traditional and familiar, yet presented in a fun, fresh way engages the learner.

We start with floating off-the-staff notes as well as notes on the staff. The pacing is graded in a manner that the note reading will not be overwhelming and the note names are placed inside the noteheads as an aide and phase out quickly as we focus on note reading building one note at a time with exercises and pieces using only the notes we have learned. The advantage of having a printed book to send home with learners helps everyone remember what and how to practice and even young children are often able to practice these without help after the first few lessons. You may use this book as a pre-cursor to method books like Suzuki Violin Book 1 or in conjunction.

In this book you will find many
tools to help your students learn the Violin including
FUN songs and worksheets!

Pieces in this book are fun to play in group lessons as well!
Students who have successfully completed this book can look forward to more skills to learn and fun pieces to master in ***A Very Fun Violin Collection***
available on Amazon

DO`S AND DON`TS FOR VIOLIN:

WASH YOUR HANDS BEFORE YOU PLAY OR PRACTICE VIOLIN.

PLACE YOUR MUSIC ON THE STAND BEFORE YOU OPEN YOUR VIOLIN CASE.

HOLD YOUR BOW WITH THE FROG OR STICK. AVOID TOUCHING THE HAIR. NATURAL OILS ON CLEAN HANDS CAN RUB OFF ON YOUR BOW WHICH PREVENTS ROSIN FROM STICKING TO YOUR BOW.

WHEN TUNING YOUR VIOLIN USE THE FINE TUNERS FOR SMALL PITCH CHANGES.

REMEMBER RIGHTY TIGHTY FOR THE PITCH TO GO HIGHER AND LEFTY LOOSEY FOR THE PITCH TO GO LOWER.

DON'T LET YOUR VIOLIN "WIGGLE" BACK AND FORTH WHEN YOU PLAY. YOUR VIOLIN SHOULD STAY STILL AND FLAT AS A TABLETOP. THE VIOLIN IS THE CONSTANT AND THE BOW IS THE VARIABLE.

ROSIN YOUR BOW A LOT WHEN IT`S BRAND NEW. IN THE FUTURE, JUST THREE SWIPES UP AND DOWN BEFORE YOU PRACTICE EACH DAY IS ENOUGH.

DON'T HOLD YOUR BOW LIKE THIS:

DO USE A MUSIC STAND!
IT WILL HELP YOU HOLD YOUR VIOLIN CORRECTLY-FLAT LIKE A TABLE AND YOU`LL SOUND BETTER!

SET UP YOUR VIOLIN WITH FINGERING TAPES:

Full Size Violin (4/4)
Tape 1 – 35mm (1 3/8 inches)
Tape 2 – 66mm (2 5/8 inches)
Tape 3 – 80mm (3 1/8 inches)
Tape 4 – 106mm (4 1/8 inches)

3/4 Violin
Tape 1 – 32mm (1 1/4 inches)
Tape 2 – 61mm (2 3/8 inches)
Tape 3 – 75 mm (2 7/8 inches)
Tape 4 – 100 mm (3 7/8 inches)

1/4 Violin
Tape 1 – 25mm (1 inch)
Tape 2 – 48mm (1 7/8 inches)
Tape 3 – 60mm (2 3/8 inches)
Tape 4 – 79mm (3 1/8 inches)

1/2 Violin
Tape 1 – 28mm (1 1/8 inches)
Tape 2 – 54mm (2 1/8 inches)
Tape 3 – 68mm (2 5/8 inches)
Tape 4 – 91mm (3 5/8 inches)

You can put a finger tape on your Violin for every finger but you only need two tapes- one for finger #1 in the natural position and one for finger #3. Finger two ALWAYS snuggles up next to finger three in this book. The above chart will help you determine where to place each tape on your specific size violin!
Measure from below the nut -see the above arrow for where to start.

WHOLE NOTE

"WHOLE NOTE HOLD IT"
4 BEATS

HALF NOTE

"HOLD ME"
2 BEATS

QUARTER NOTE

"QUARTER"
1 BEAT

EIGHTH NOTES

TWO 8TH NOTES =
1 QUARTER NOTE

FERMATA

HOLD NOTES LONGER
THAN NORMAL

SHARP

RAISE PITCH BY
A HALF STEP

FLAT

LOWER PITCH BY
A HALF STEP

TREBLE CLEF

G CLEF
TREBLE NOTES

WHOLE REST

HOLD 4 BEATS

HALF REST

HOLD 2 BEATS

QUARTER REST

HOLD 1 BEAT

REPEAT SIGN

PLAY AGAIN

DOUBLE BAR LINE

THE END OF THE
PIECE

STAFF

5 LINES
4 SPACES

BAR LINE

DIVIDES STAFF
INTO MEASURES

DOTTED HALF NOTE

"HOLD ME PLEASE"
THREE BEATS

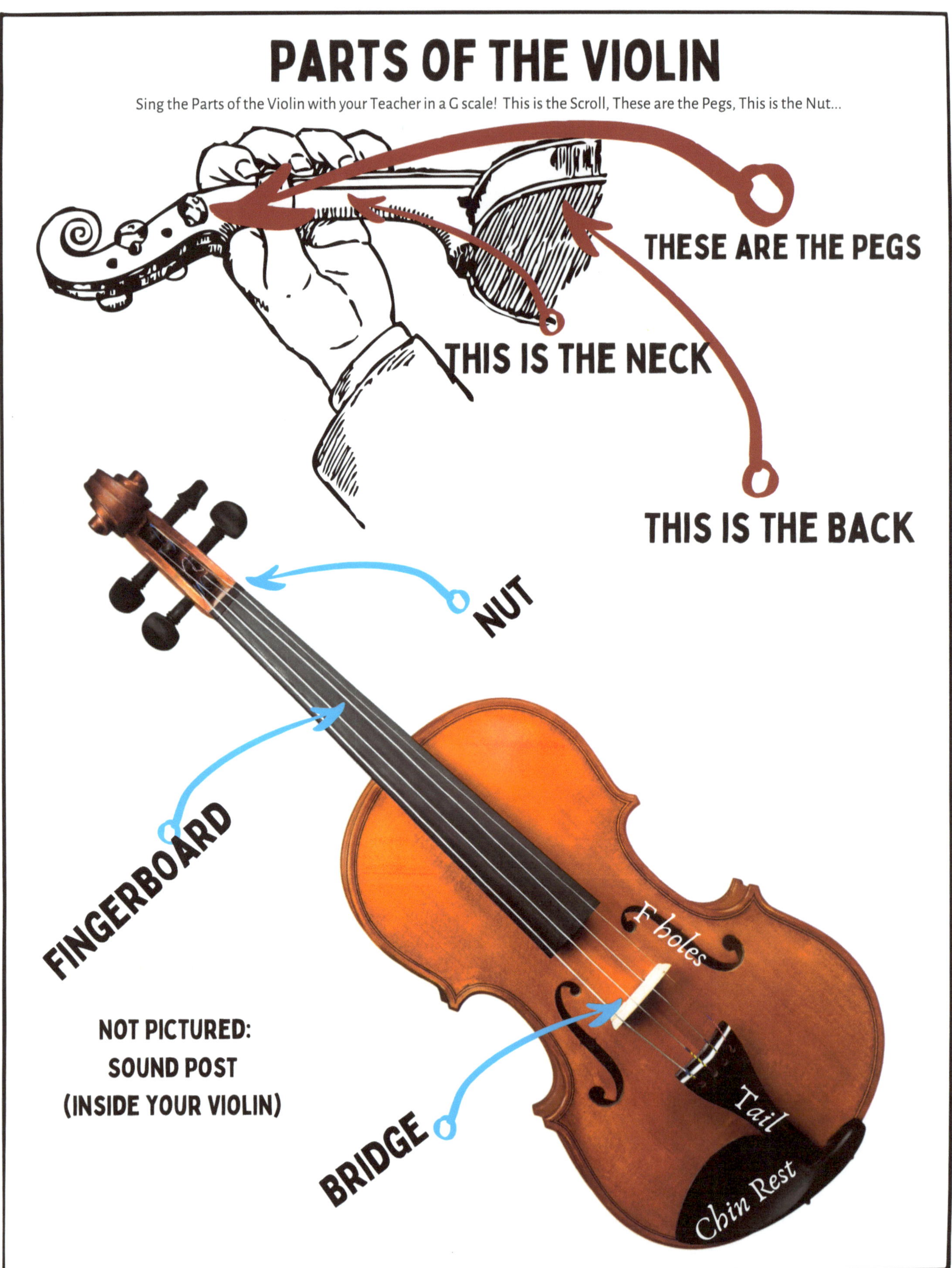
PARTS OF THE VIOLIN
Sing the Parts of the Violin with your Teacher in a G scale! This is the Scroll, These are the Pegs, This is the Nut...
THESE ARE THE PEGS
THIS IS THE NECK
THIS IS THE BACK
NUT
FINGERBOARD
F holes
NOT PICTURED:
SOUND POST
(INSIDE YOUR VIOLIN)
BRIDGE
Tail
Chin Rest

DOWN IN THE VALLEY

ARRANGED BY
MRS. JUDY NAILLON
"VIOLINJUDY"

TRADITIONAL

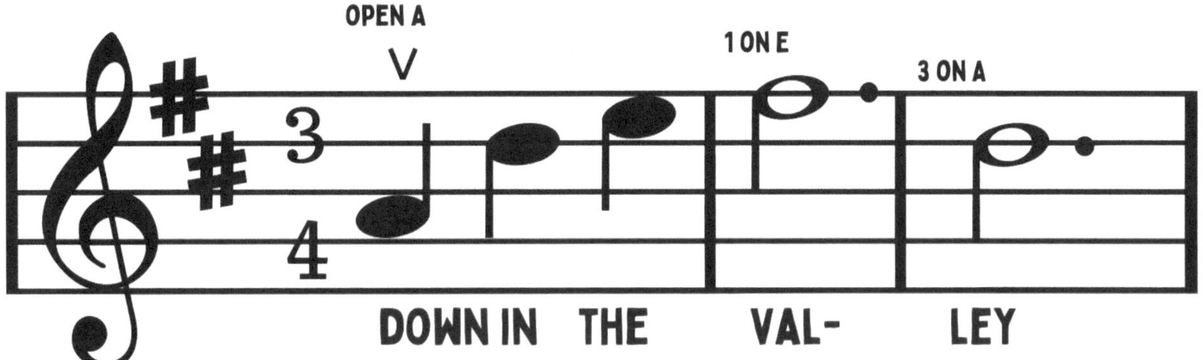

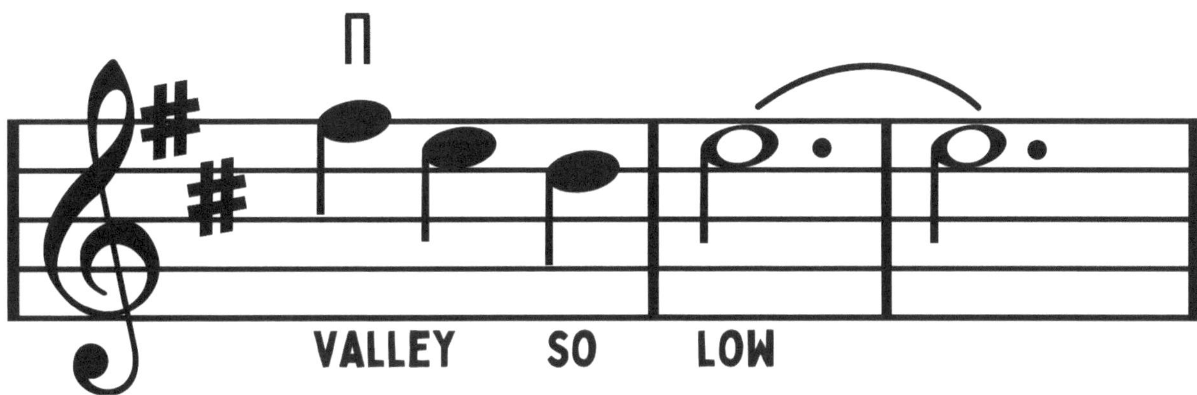

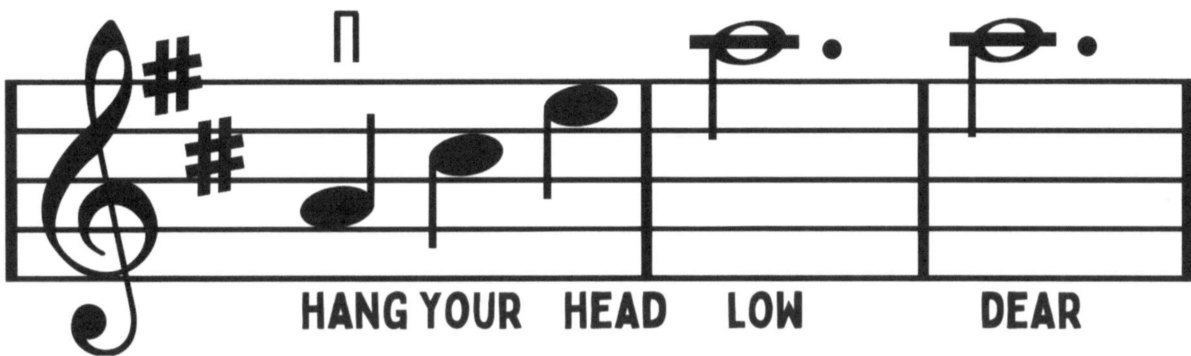

ARRANGED BY
MRS. JUDY NAILLON
"VIOLINJUDY"
MY BONNIE LIES OVER THE OCEAN
TRADITIONAL
OPEN A
MY BONNIE LIES OVER THE
O- CEAN MY BONNIE LIES
O - VER THE SEA MY
BON - NIE LIES OV- ER THE
OCEAN OH BRING BACK MY

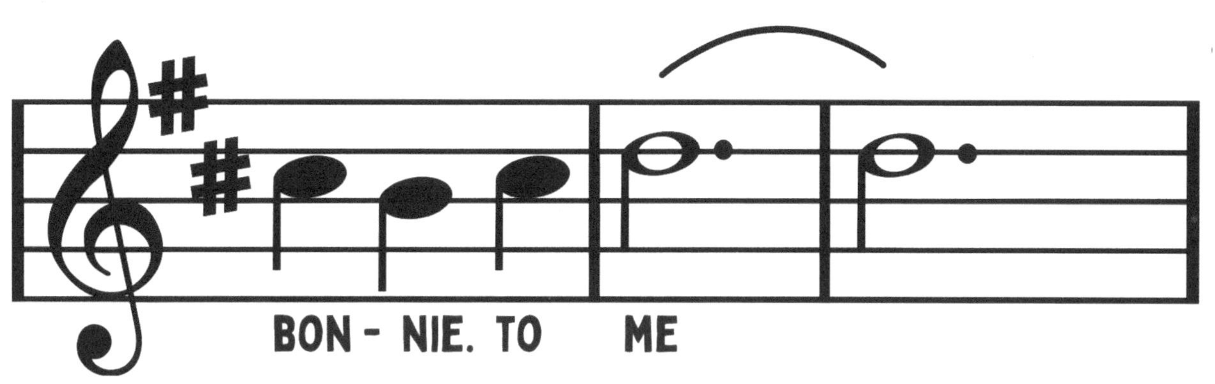
BON - NIE. TO
ME

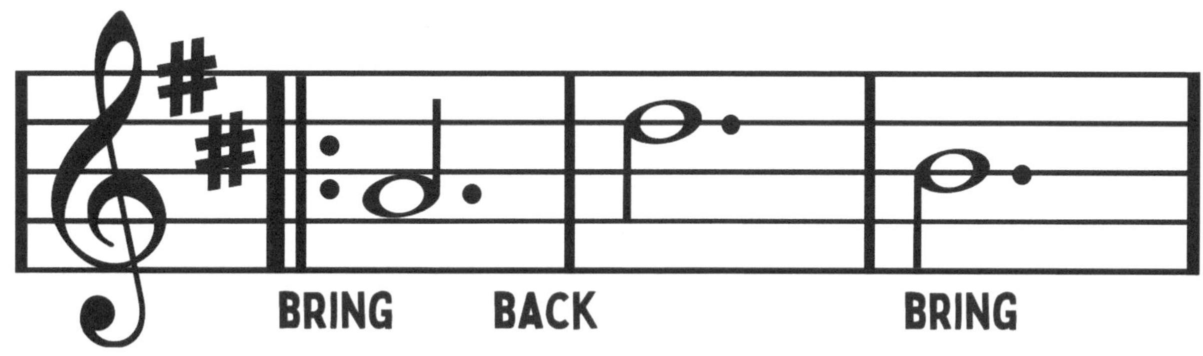
BRING
BACK
BRING

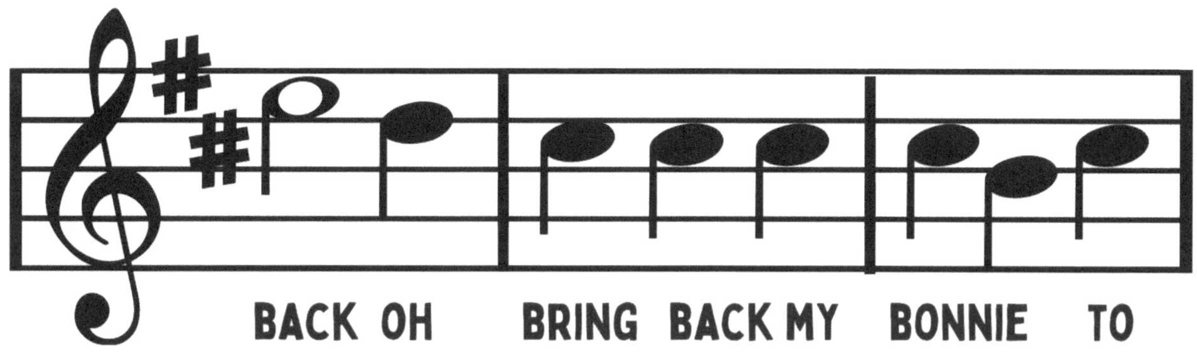
BACK OH
BRING BACK MY
BONNIE TO

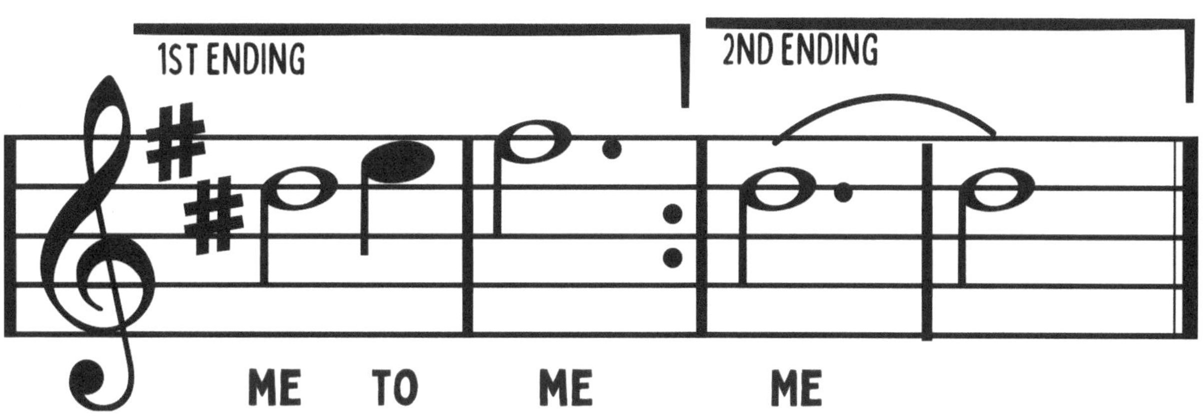
1ST ENDING
2ND ENDING
ME TO
ME
ME

BICYCLE BUILT FOR TWO

ARRANGED BY
MRS. JUDY NAILLON
"VIOLINJUDY"

HARRY DACRE

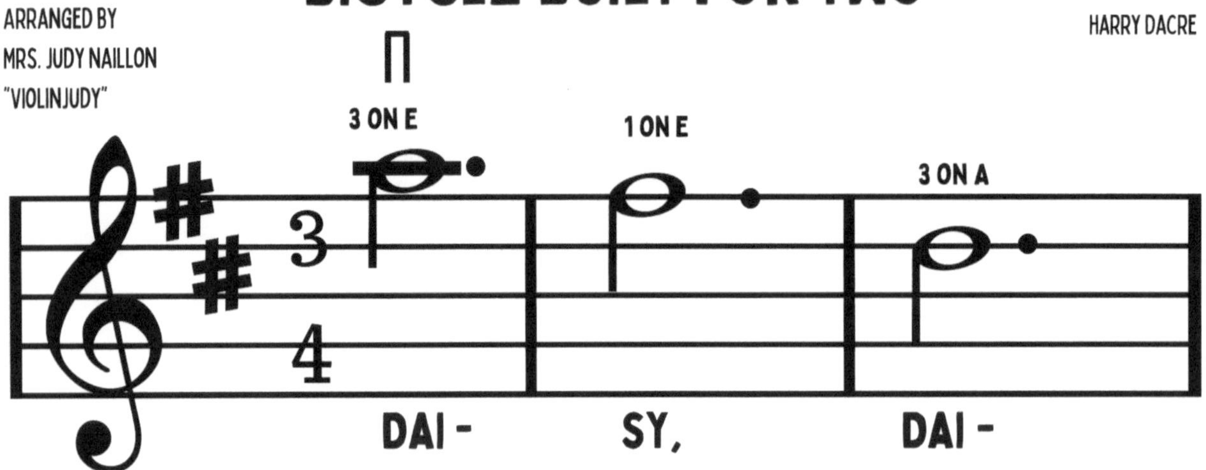

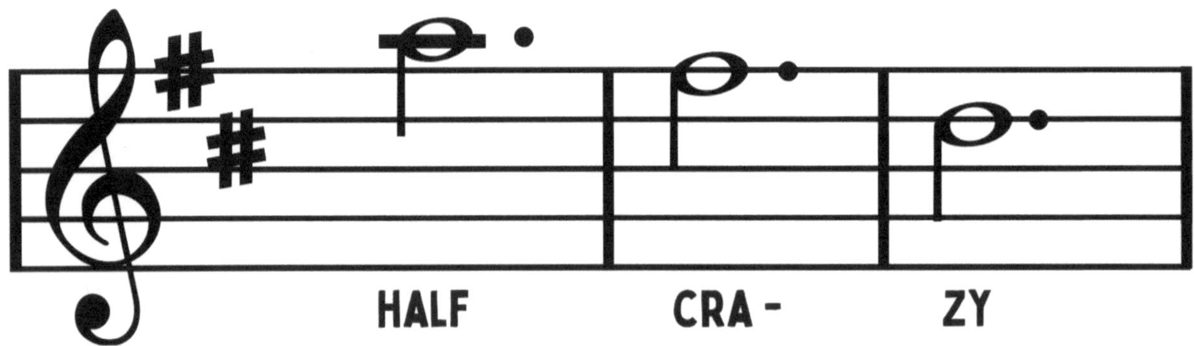

ALL FOR THE. LOVE OF YOU

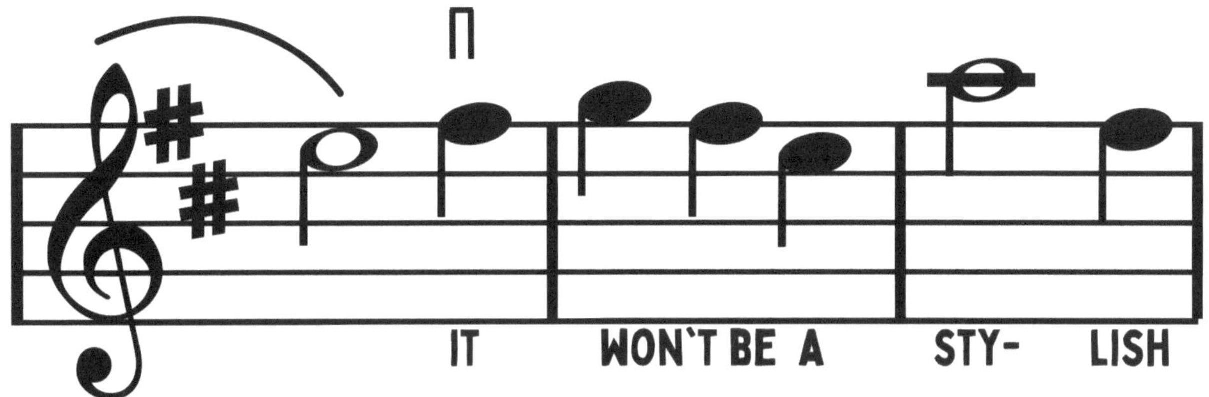
IT WON'T BE A STY- LISH

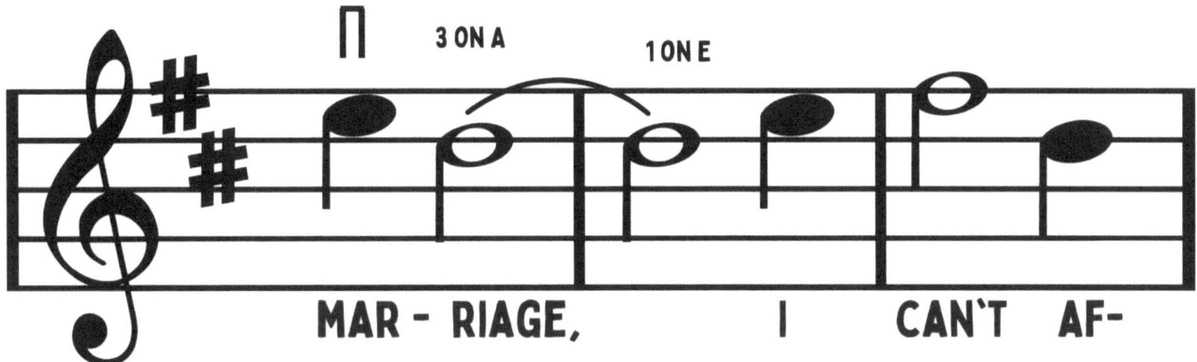
3 ON A
1 ON E
MAR - RIAGE, I CAN'T AF-

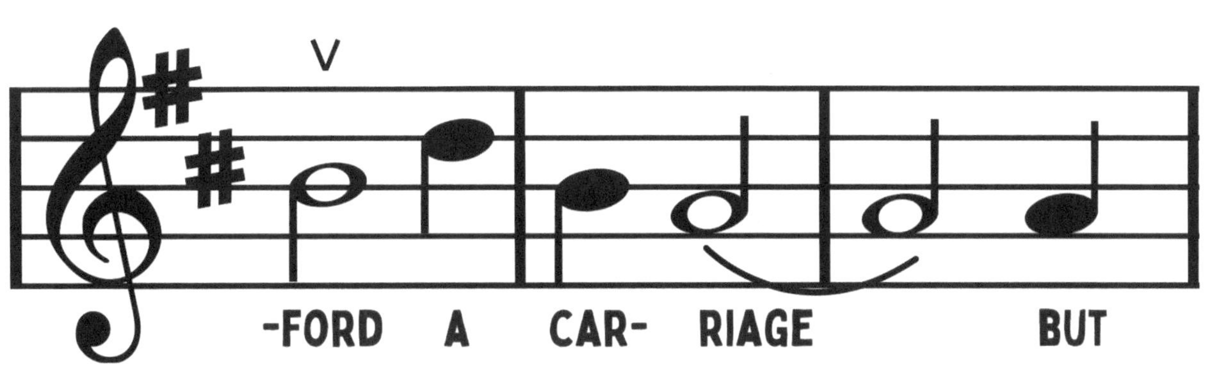
-FORD A CAR- RIAGE BUT

YOU'LL LOOK SWEET UP - ON A

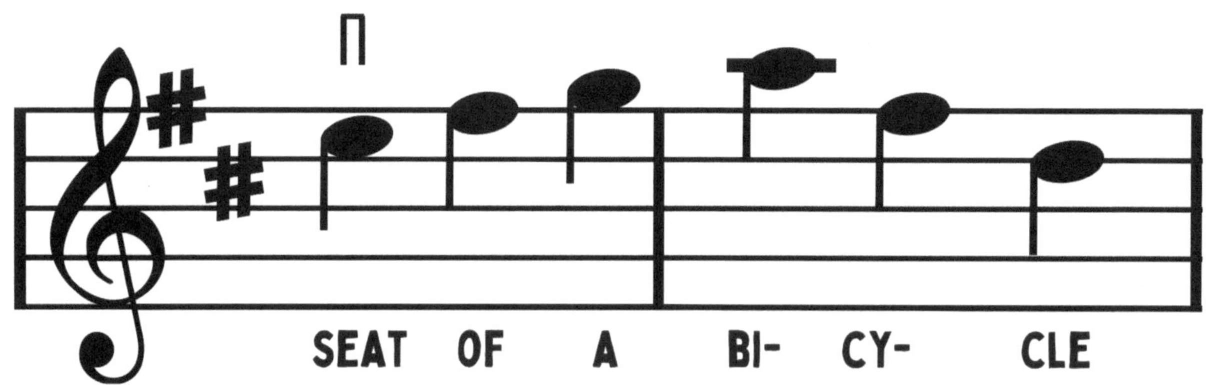
SEAT OF A BI- CY- CLE

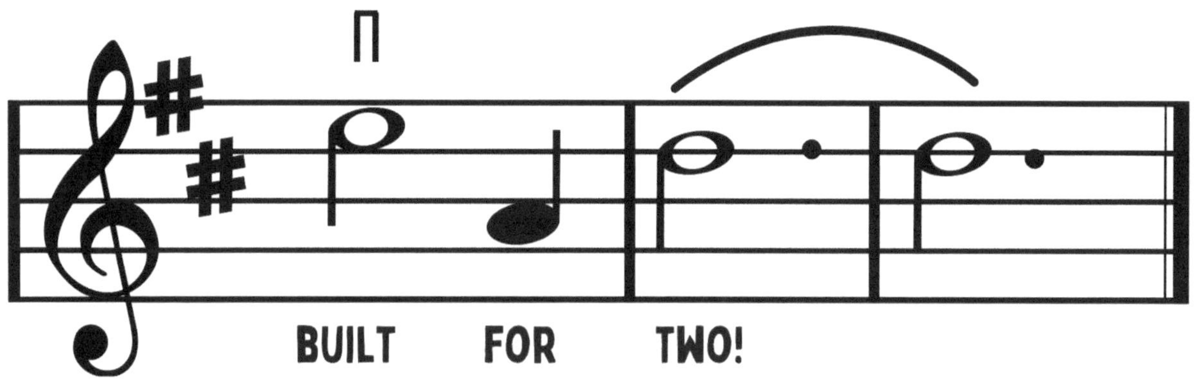
BUILT FOR TWO!

TAKE ME OUT TO THE BALLGAME

ARRANGED BY
MRS. JUDY NAILLON
"VIOLINJUDY"

NORWORTH &
BAYES

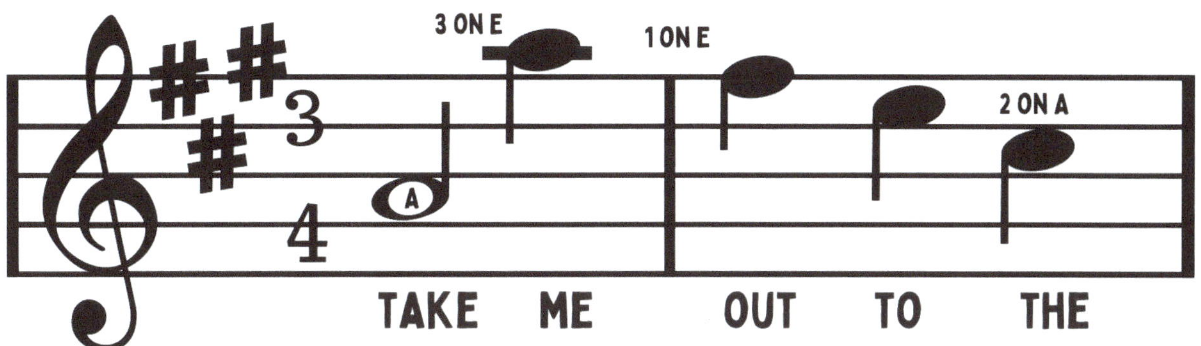

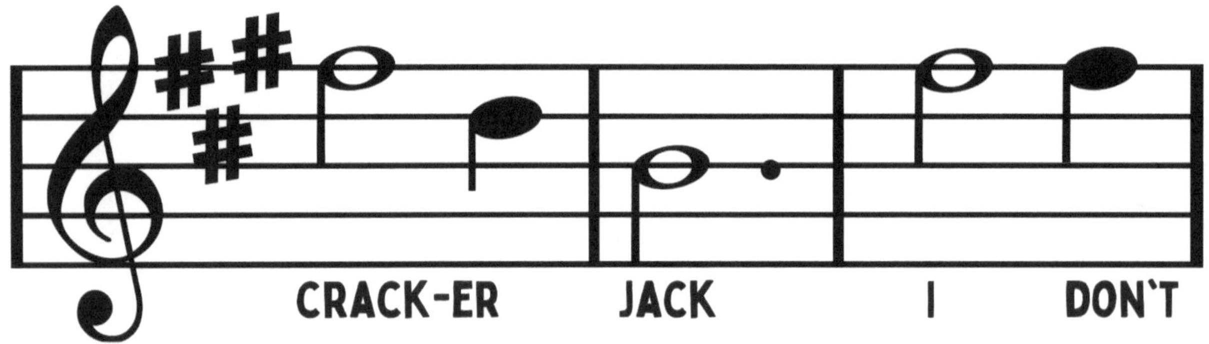
CRACK-ER JACK I DON'T

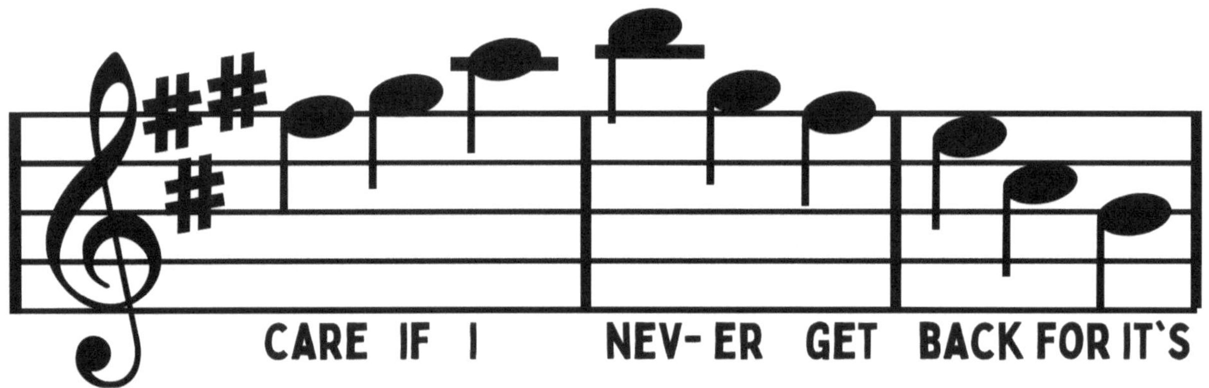
CARE IF I NEV- ER GET BACK FOR IT'S

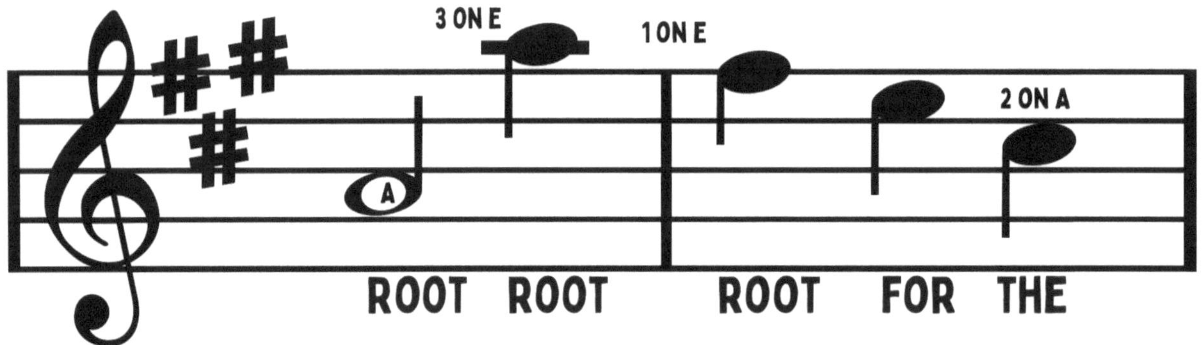
3 ON E
1 ON E
A
2 ON A
ROOT ROOT ROOT FOR THE

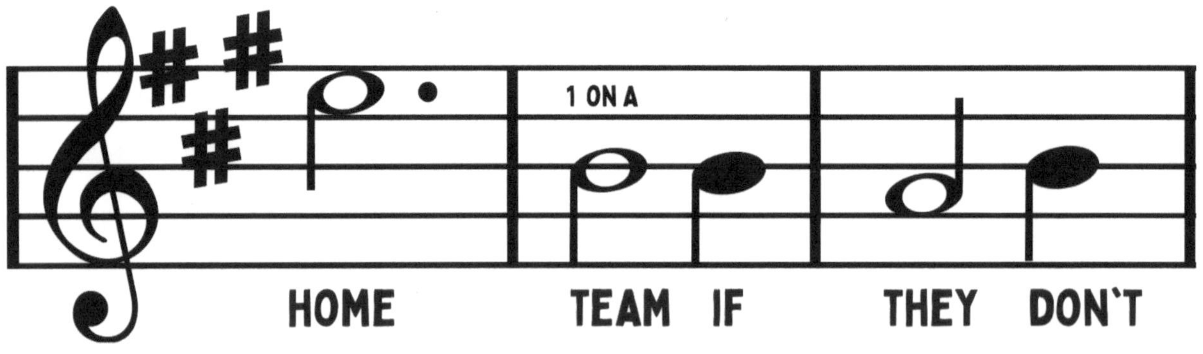
1 ON A
HOME TEAM IF THEY DON'T

WIN IT'S A SHAME FOR IT'S

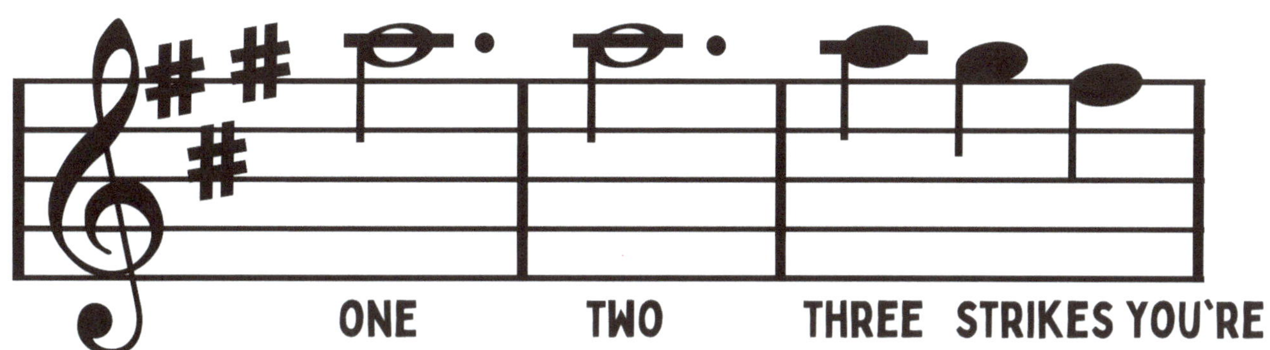
ONE TWO THREE STRIKES YOU'RE

OUT AT THE OLD BALL
GAME!

THREE CORNERED HAT

ARRANGED BY
MRS. JUDY NAILLON
"VIOLINJUDY"

TRADITIONAL

BEAMED 8TH NOTES

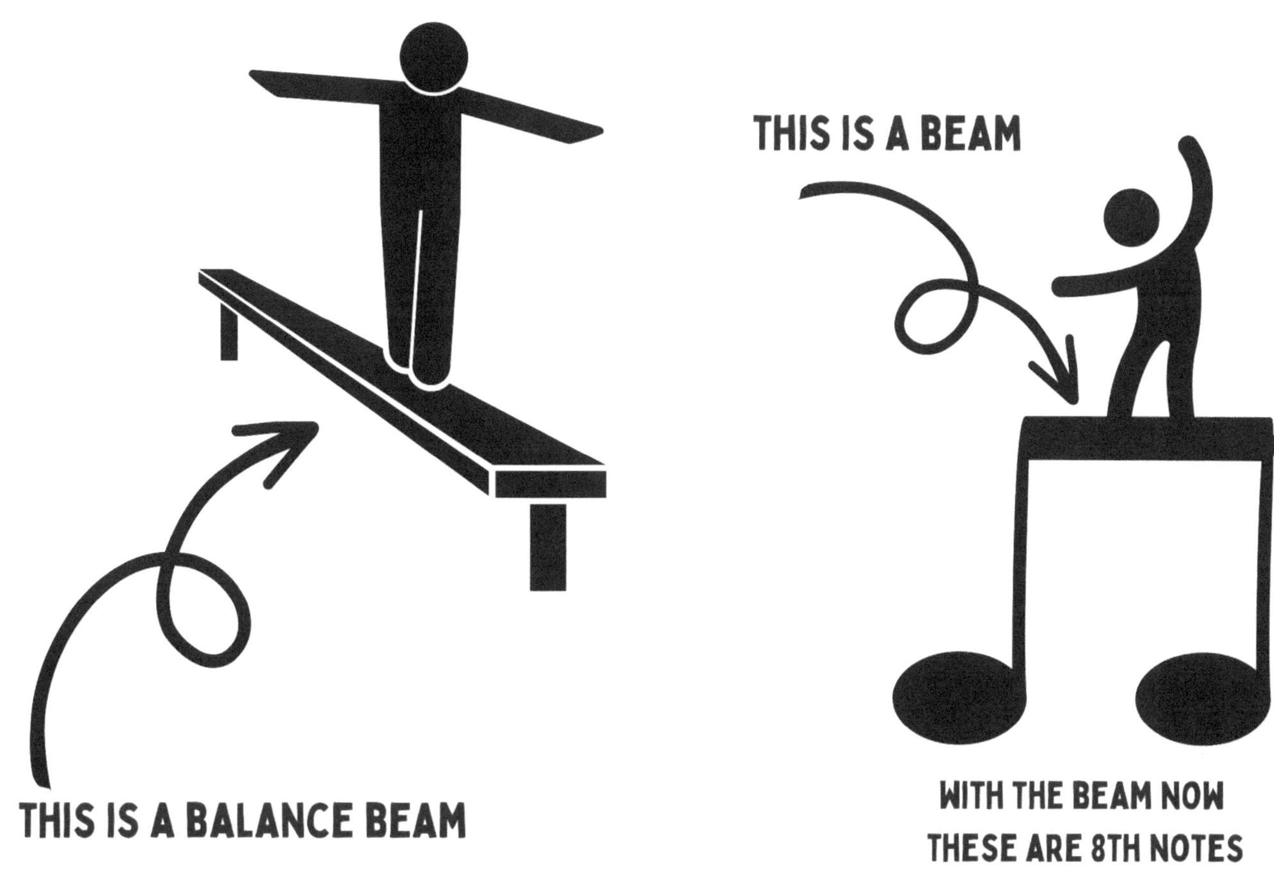

WITH THE BEAM NOW
THESE ARE 8TH NOTES

IN MUSIC SOMETIMES NOTES HAVE A BEAM, THIS IS A LINE THAT CONNECTS THE STEMS TOGETHER. THIS IS SECRET CODE FOR FASTER NOTES! BUT HOW MUCH FASTER DO WE PLAY THESE NOTES? TWICE AS FAST AS A QUARTER NOTE. WHEN YOU SEE A QUARTER NOTE THINK "WALK" AND WHEN YOU SEE EITGHTH NOTES THINK "RUNNING"

TO HELP YOU REMEMBER TO PLAY BEAMED NOTES FASTER, WE HAVE REPLACED THE BEAMS WITH RUNNING BUNNIES IN THE NEXT PIECE- WHEN YOU SEE THE BUNNIES PLAY RUNNING-FASTER NOTES!

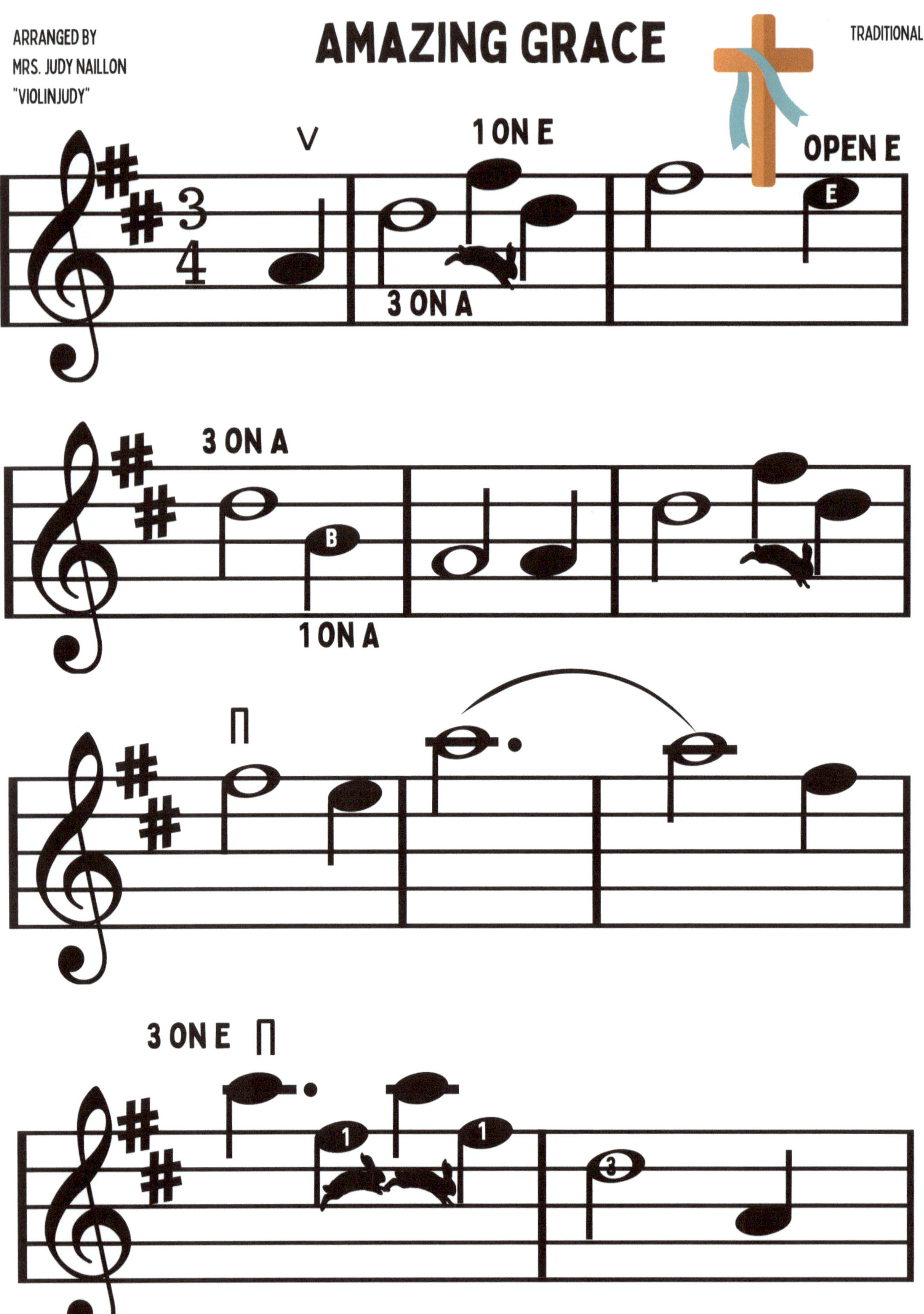
ARRANGED BY
MRS. JUDY NAILLON
"VIOLINJUDY"
AMAZING GRACE
TRADITIONAL
V
1 ON E
OPEN E
E
3 ON A
3 ON A
B
1 ON A
⊓
3 ON E
⊓
1
1
3

LYRICS:

AMAZING GRACE, HOW SWEET THE SOUND

THAT SAVED A WRETCH LIKE ME

I ONCE WAS LOST BUT NOW AM FOUND

WAS BLIND BUT NOW I SEE

LAVENDER`S BLUE

ARRANGED BY
MRS. JUDY NAILLON
"VIOLINJUDY"

NORWORTH &
BAYES

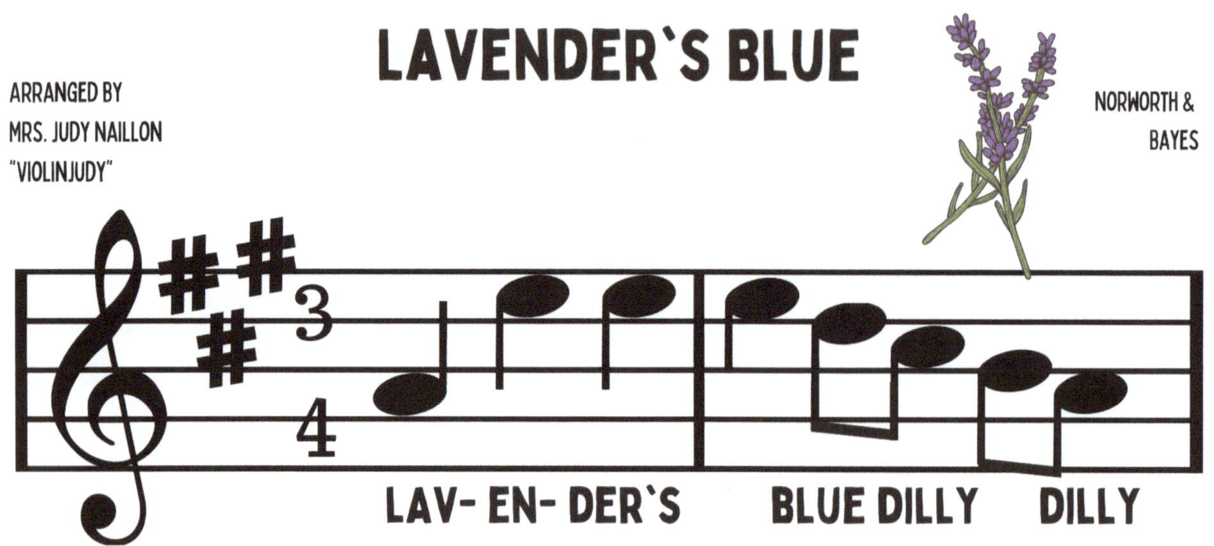

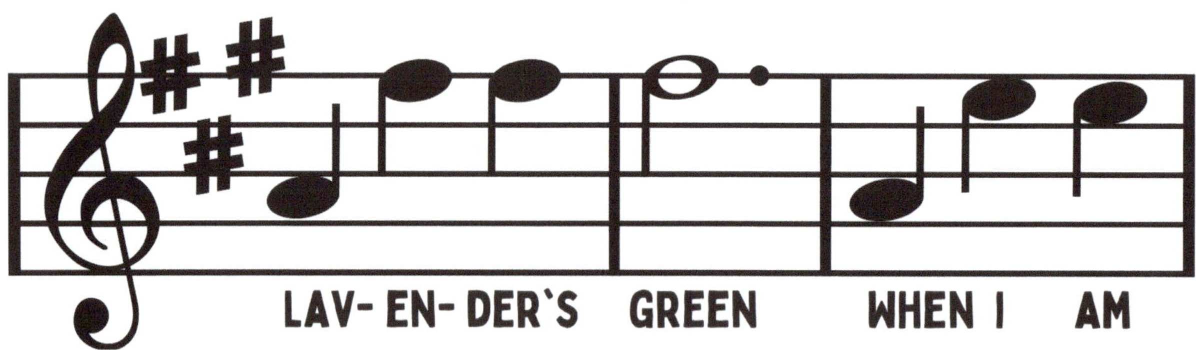

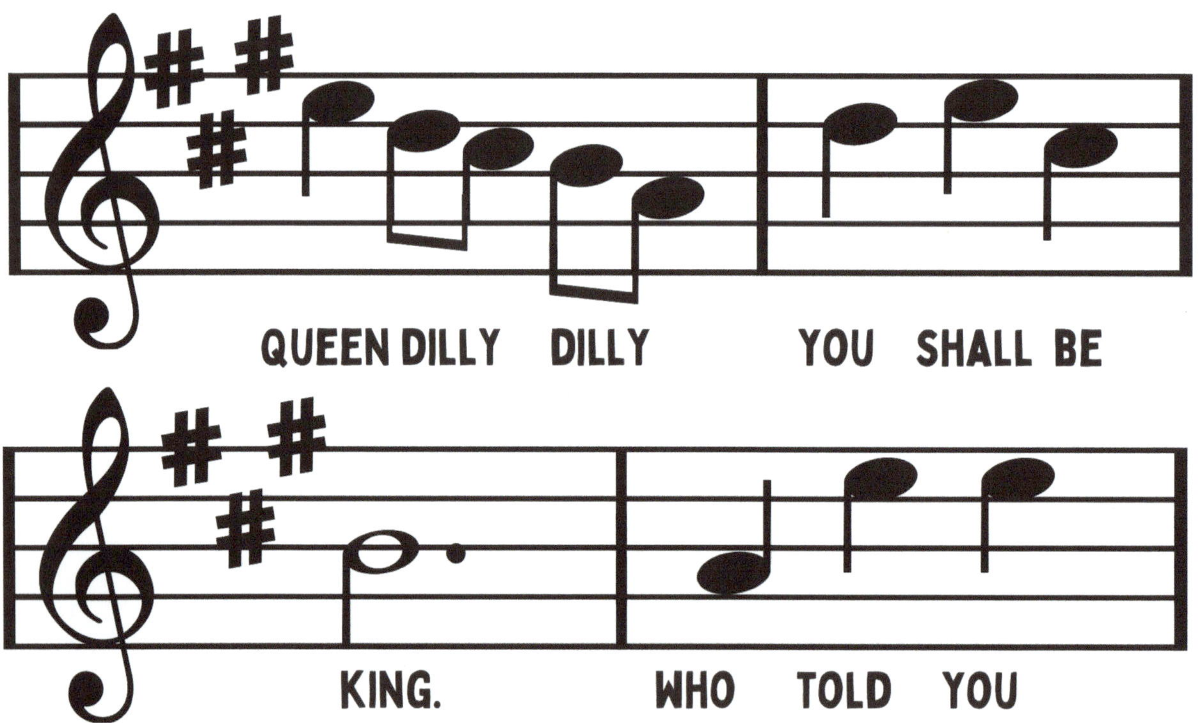

SO DILLY DILLY WHO TOLD YOU

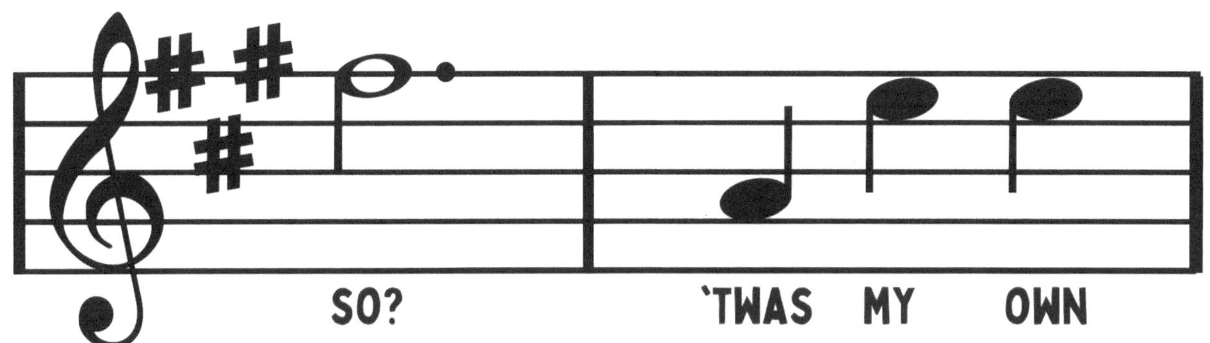
SO? `TWAS MY OWN

HEART DILLY DILLY, THAT TOLD ME

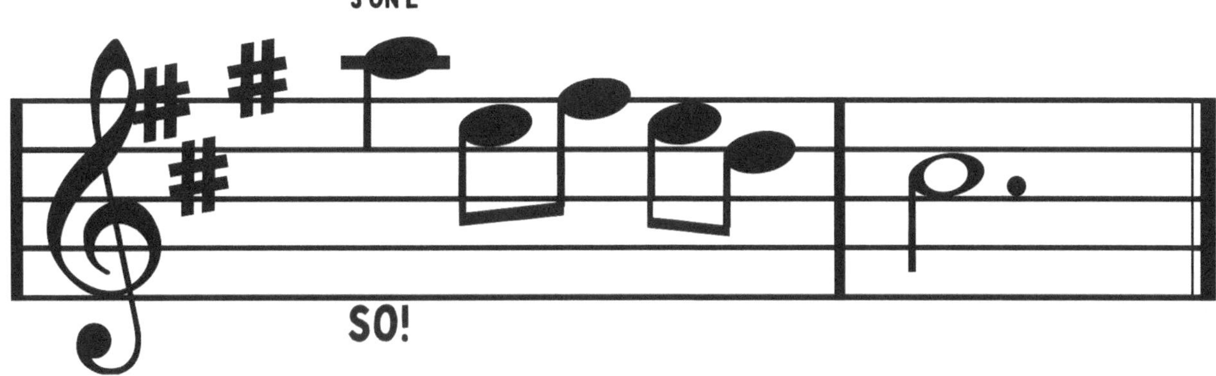
3 ON E
SO!

SPANISH DANCE
TCHAIKOVSKY
LOW 2
LOW 2

HAPPY BIRTHDAY!

NOTICE THE NEW BEAMED EIGHTH NOTES! REMEMBER TO PLAY LOW 2 ON E!

G
A
B
C
D
E
F
G

A
B
C
D
E
F
G
A

Mrs. Judy Naillon, or "ViolinJudy" is a dedicated and enthusiastic independent piano and violin teacher, composer, and professional violinist. Her work consists of her large private music studio, as well as playing with her string quartet and Wichita Symphony Orchestra. She served as a church musician for over 20 years and is active in leadership in the musicians' union. She loves coming up with creative ideas to help both students and teachers be successful and blogs about it all at www.ViolinJudy.com and for Alfred's Music Publishers. When she is not writing new Violin books she loves spending time with her family and little dog Pom.

BOOK LEVEL CHART FOR THE **VERY FUN VIOLIN LIBRARY**

VIOLIN GRADE	FUN VIOLIN LEVEL	MAIN CONCEPTS
PRE-TWINKLE	A	RHYTHMS, FINGERS 1,2,3 ON A FINGER 1 ON E
LEVEL 1A	B	NOTE READING 1,2,3 ON A OPEN D & 1 ON E
LEVEL IB	C	NOTE READING ON D, A& E STRINGS, FINGER 4
LEVEL 2A	D	NOTE READING ON ALL STRINGS
LEVEL 2B	E	INTRO TO 3RD POSITION & VIBRATO

CERTIFICATE

OF ACHIEVEMENT

This awarded to :

_ _ _ _ _ _ _ _ _ _ _ _ _ _ _ _ _

for the achievement of the completion of:

_ _ _ _ _ _ _ _ _ _ _ _ _ _ _ _ _

Teacher

Date

www.ingramcontent.com/pod-product-compliance
Lightning Source LLC
LaVergne TN
LVHW070159110826
845147LV00002B/444
* 9 7 8 1 9 6 0 6 7 4 1 5 9 *